The Doodle Book

187 Fun Drawings You Can Finish Yourself

JOHN M. DUGGAN

Ulysses Press

Published by:
ULYSSES PRESS
P.O. Box 3440
Berkeley, CA 94703
www.ulyssespress.com

ISBN10: 1-56975-676-7
ISBN13: 978-1-56975-676-8
Library of Congress Control Number 2008904139

Printed in Canada by Transcontinental Printing

10 9 8 7 6 5 4 3 2 1

Acquisitions Editor: Nick Denton-Brown
Managing Editor: Claire Chun
Production: Tamara Kowalski
Cover design: John M. Duggan

Distributed by Publishers Group West

John M. Duggan has been in search of the "funnest" job all his life. He has worked variously as a cartoonist, illustrator, video game artist, novelist, playwright, screenwriter, director, producer, actor, singer, and double-left footed dancer hoping to find that elusive position. He's worked for companies ranging from Disney to Sony to Electronic Arts in a variety of artistic capacities. He currently lives, works, and performs in the Bay Area with his wife Kathryn and twin actor sons, Nik and Khail.

What's chasing the butterfly queen?

What's headed toward Earth?

Who's fighting Sir Dragonfly?

Are you a graffiti artist?

Shakespeare needs a play to direct.

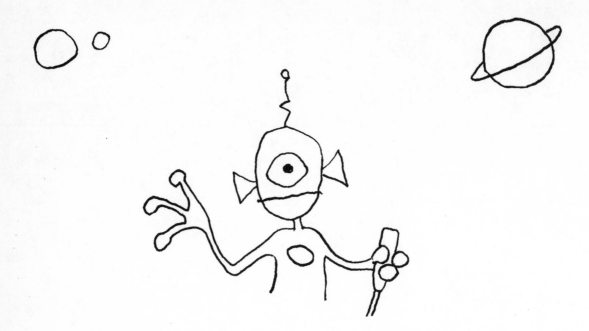

It's the newest alien hovercraft.

Give Mr. Squirrel his dream home.

What do the gnomes build at their factory?

It's no soft landing for Cowboy Bob!

It's the big vegetable head family.

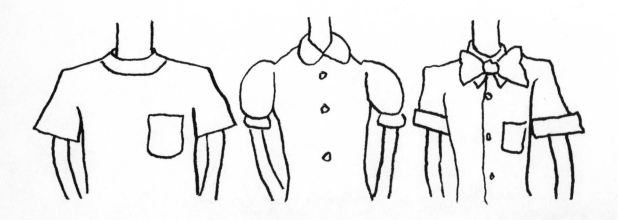

Sam the Driver gives rides to some strange creatures.

What a thrilling circus act!

What's chasing the cat?

How many clowns can you fit in the clown car?

Make a puppet show.

Who's looking out the window?

What's in the scientist's microscope?

The puppet master needs some puppets.

Vera the Vegetable Vendor needs a variety of veggies.

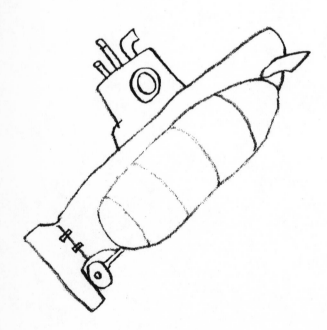

Man the battlestations. Aaoogah! Something's attacking!

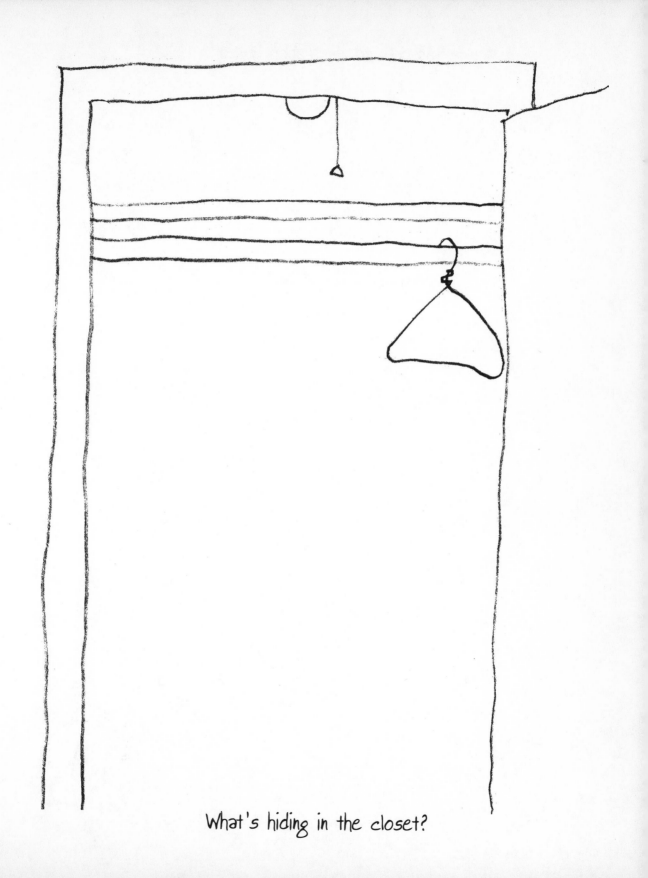

What's hiding in the closet?

All bow to the rabbit queen!

MMM! What's your favorite pizza?

Samantha sells all sorts of sushi.

What's Tokyo Sam selling?

How did the fisherman catch that?!

What would you sail the stormy seas in?

Make a super-plane that can beat the stormy skies.

What's hiding in the desert?

To the center of the Earth!

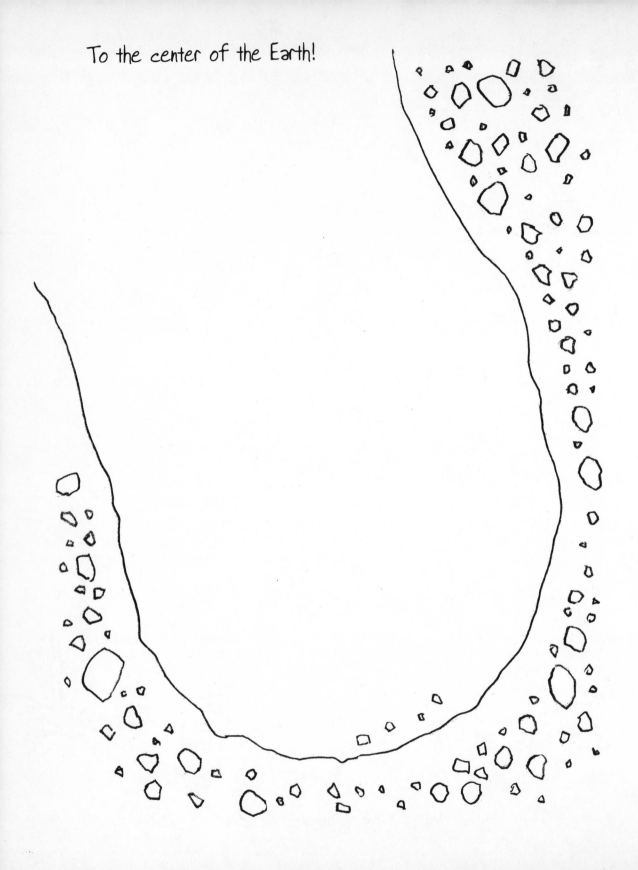

Why is she so happy?

Why is he so mad?

Who's chasing Jack?

Wow! It's a whatchamacallit!

Draw the mad scientist's latest creation.

Decorate Buffy the Punk Rocker.

Biff wants to be cool. Give him some style!

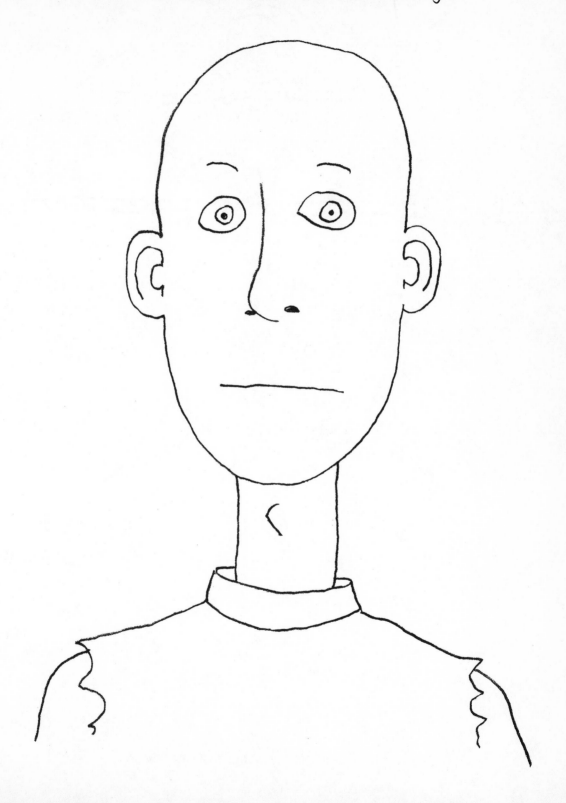

What's Tightrope Tammy walking over?

Whoops, you're not supposed to sit on that.

Decorate your wall.

It's the leprechaun's treasure!

What monster lives under the bridge?

The blacksmith made weapons for Sir Knight.

What's making the clown sad?

Make the best snowman ever.

Candymaker Carl stayed up all night to make you this.

I need some shade!

Hamster mania!

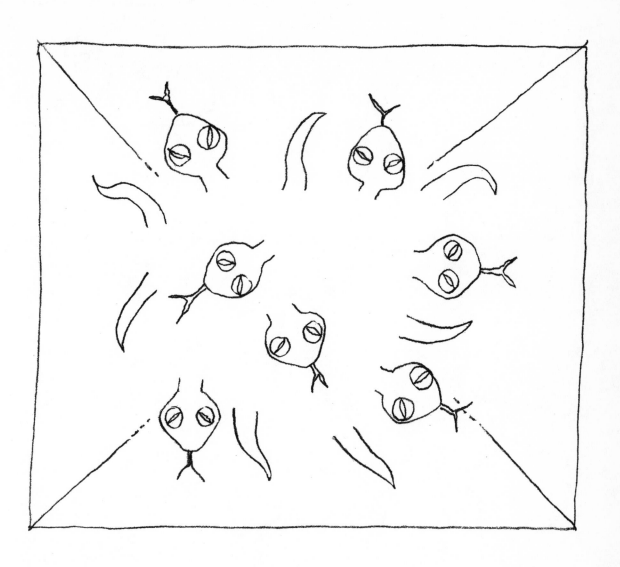

Are they snakes or lizards?

Baker Bill made this wedding cake just for you!

Too many penguins!

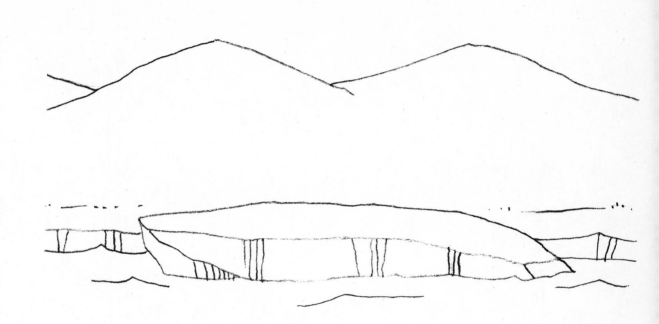

Fill the aquarium.

That's one crazy bug!

What's under the magnifying glass?

What did Pierre bake this time?

What's the circus performer balancing?

Give the snake a body.

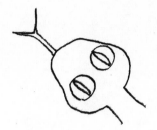

Dave is delivering something big!

That's a heavy load!

What did Explorer Frank bring home?

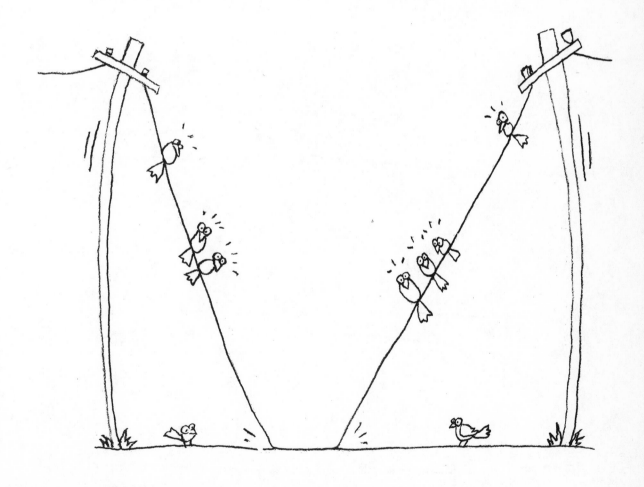

What landed on the telephone line?

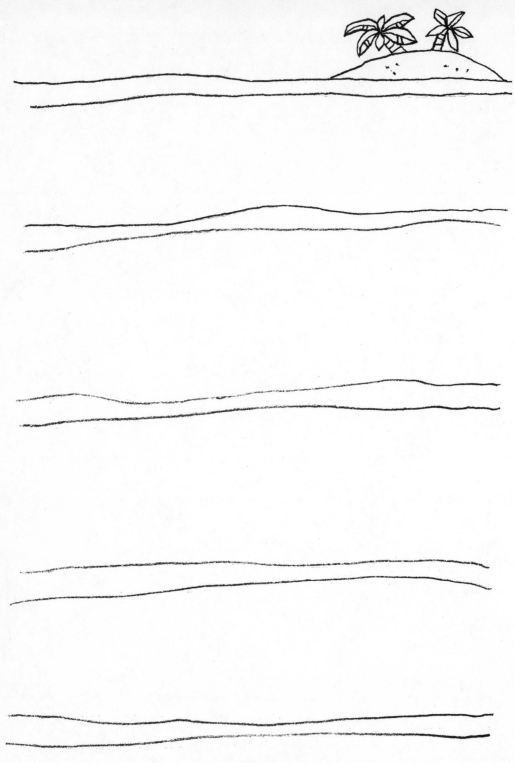

It's a beautiful day to go boating!

What a fantastic bubble sculpture!

How can I get off the island?

How many baby bunnies do Mr. and Mrs. Bunny have?

What does Jane and Tommy's invisible friend look like?

What's under the bed?

This parrot needs a fancy tail.

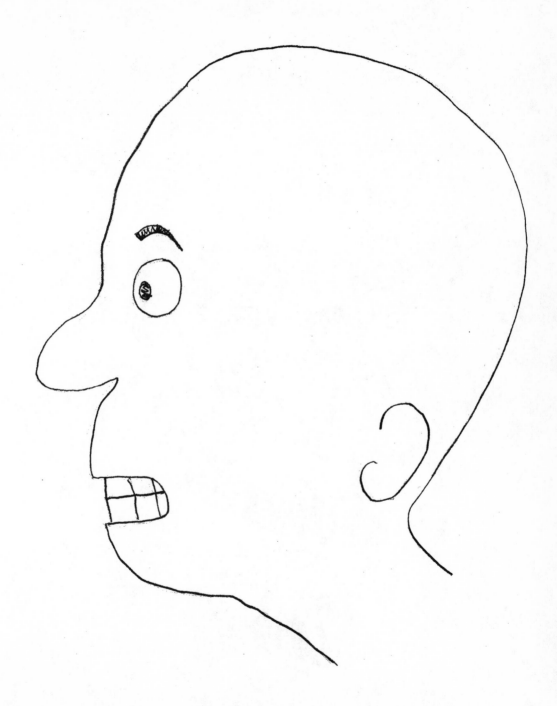

What's on your mind?

Draw Abe Lincoln's new hat.

You never know what's underwater!

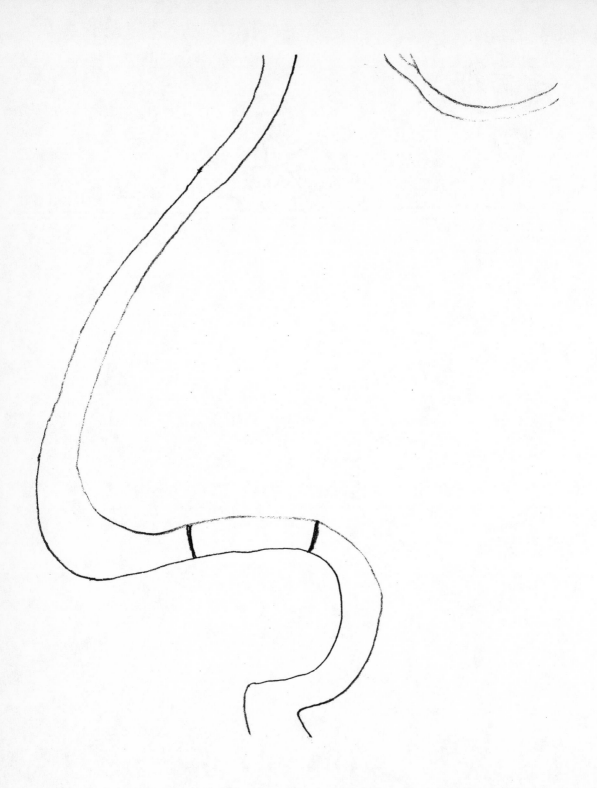

What treasures can you hide in your nose?

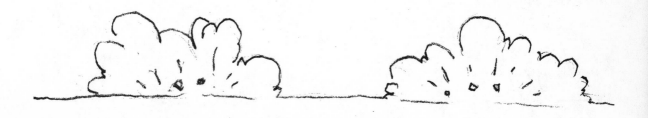

What's the ogre standing on?

Rapunzel needs some long hair.

Give the mermaid princess a fancy tail.

Fido's buried something big.

It's the biggest in the world!

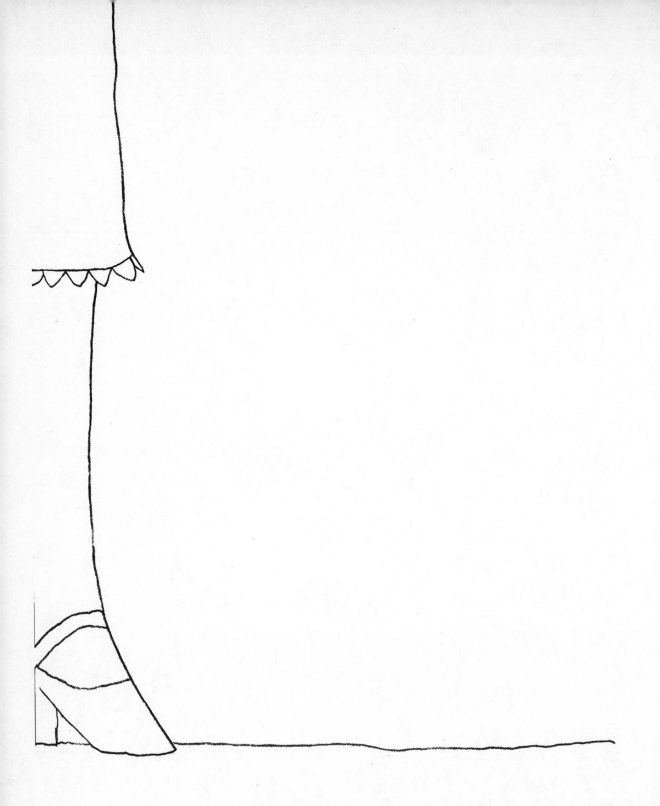

Draw life as a bug.

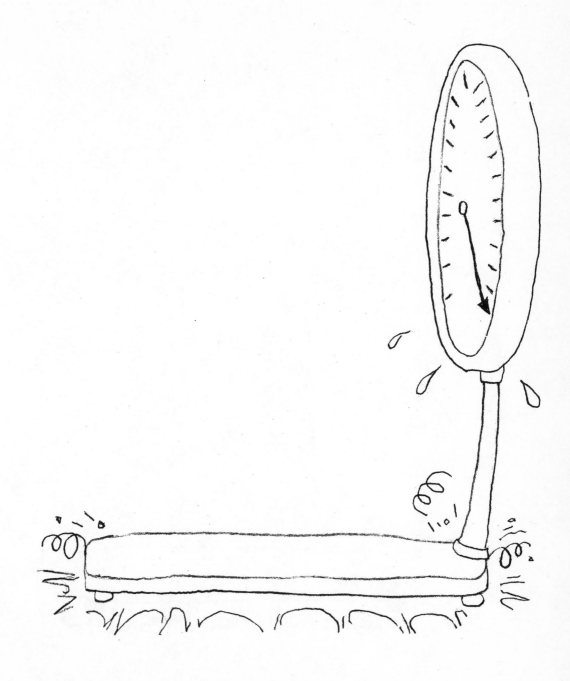

Wow! That's heavy!

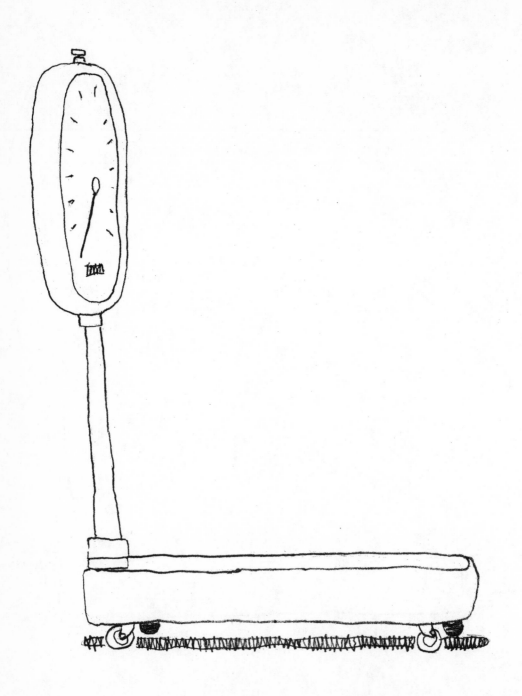

It's as light as a feather.

Astronaut Andy defends his ship!

Who's chasing Billy the Kid?

Give the samurai a challenger.

How much weight is he lifting?

Is it a beautiful flower or a carnivorous plant?

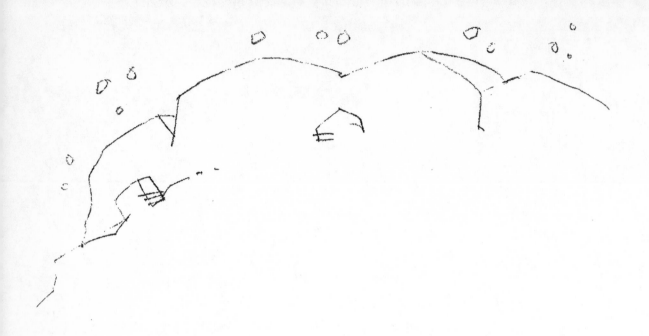

What's coming down the mountain?

Give the invisible man some clothes.

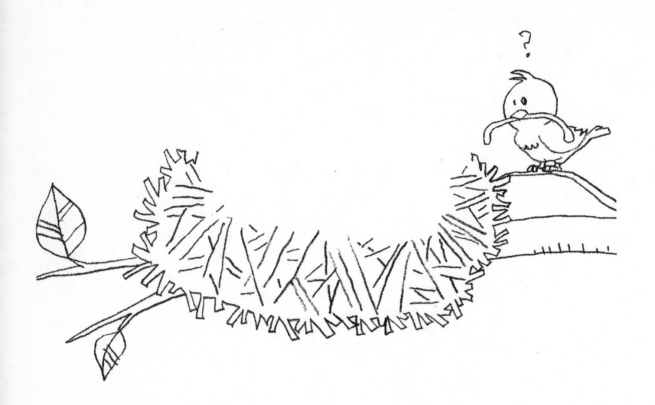

Why is mama bird so confused?

What's the circus performer juggling?

Mary the Maid battles the evil dustbunnies!

What's sneaking up behind the treasure hunter?

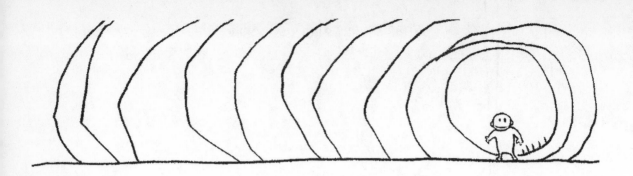

What's in the cave?

Save Tokyo!

Draw your dream castle.

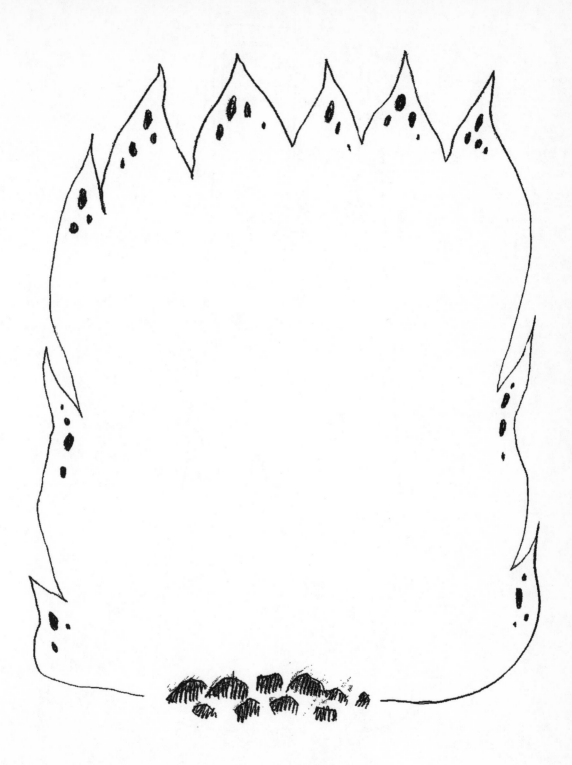

What's burning?

What's at the bottom of the well?

AIEEE! Ghosts!

Draw the ghost king.

What's bigger and badder than the Big, Bad Wolf?

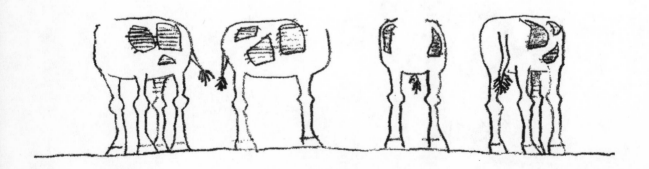

Finish the giraffes.

What's the witch riding tonight?

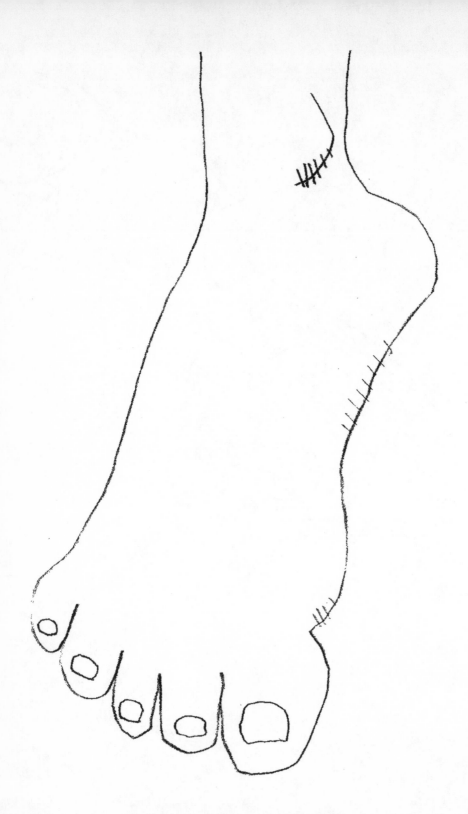

Winner of the scariest foot contest.

How'd she get up there?

Whoa! Moon monsters!

Catch that bug!

Your icky dinner is served.

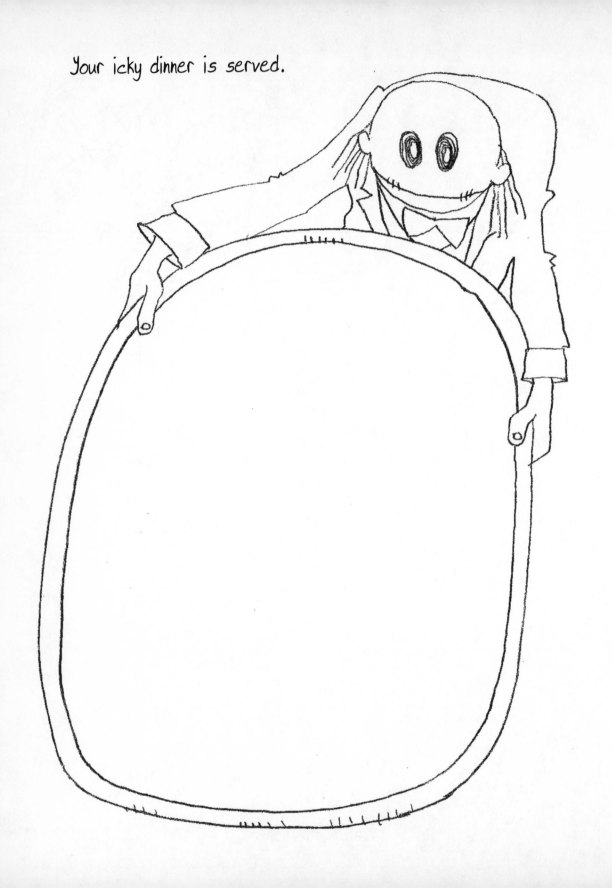

EEK! It got me!!

Draw a dolphin playground.

What did the x-ray show?

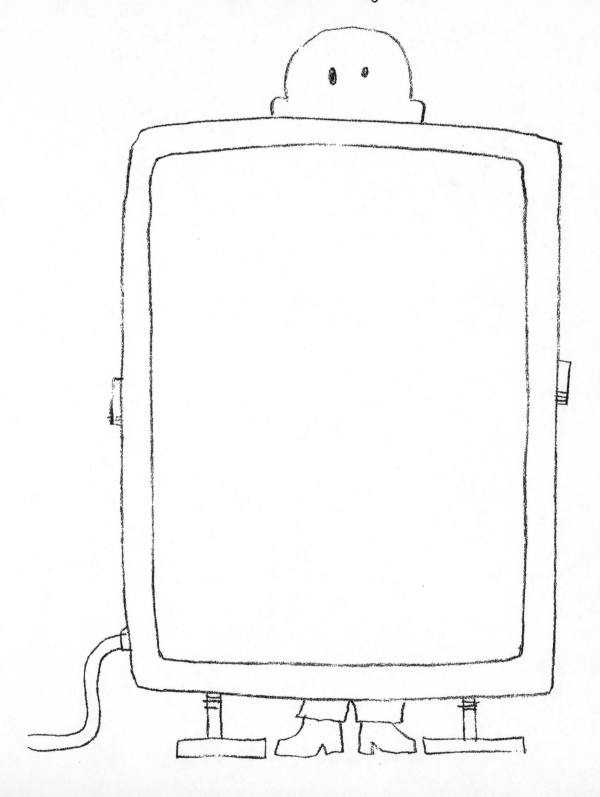

Presenting Mr. Longlegs and Mrs. Bigfoot.

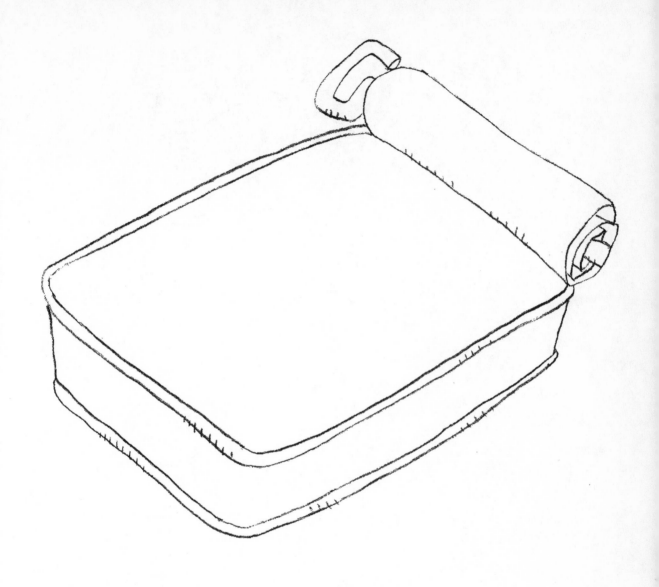

What's packed in the can?

Help Henry make a huge house of cards.

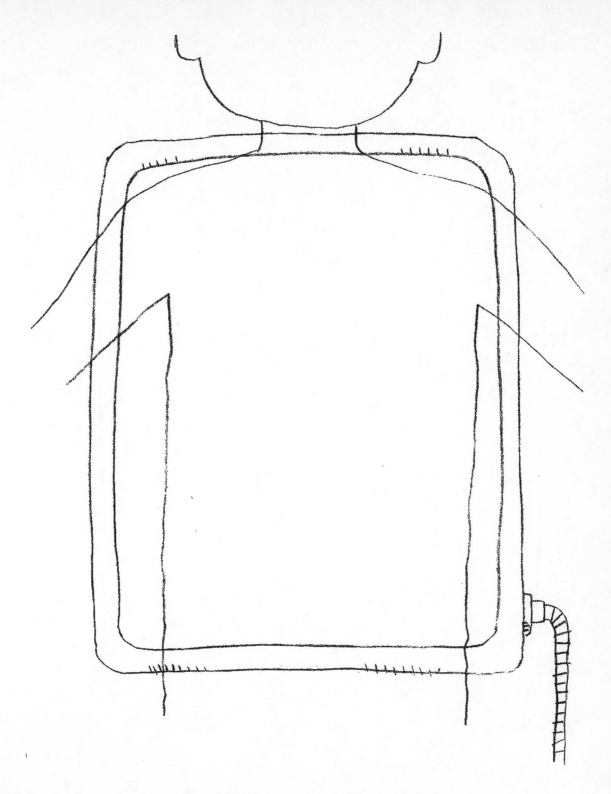

What did he eat for dinner?

The Poledome people decorated their heads in interesting ways.

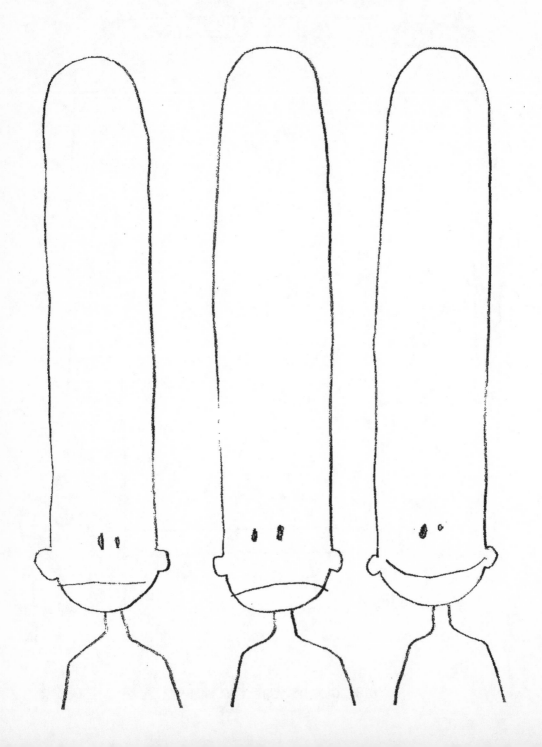

It's the soda pop genie!

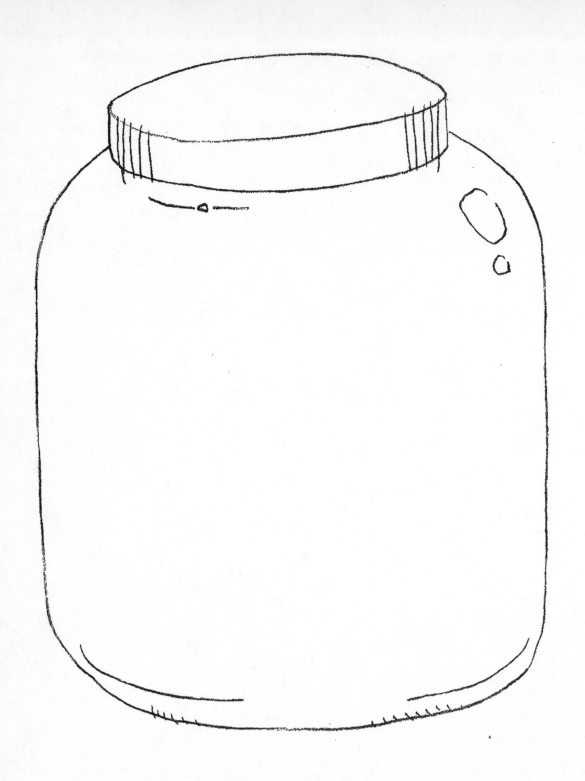

What's in the jar?

What came out of the magic egg?

What did Henrietta lay?

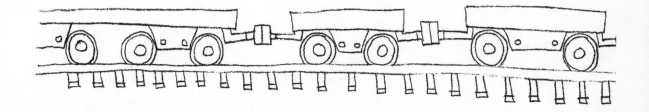

I've never seen a train carry THOSE before!

Give the plant some flowers.

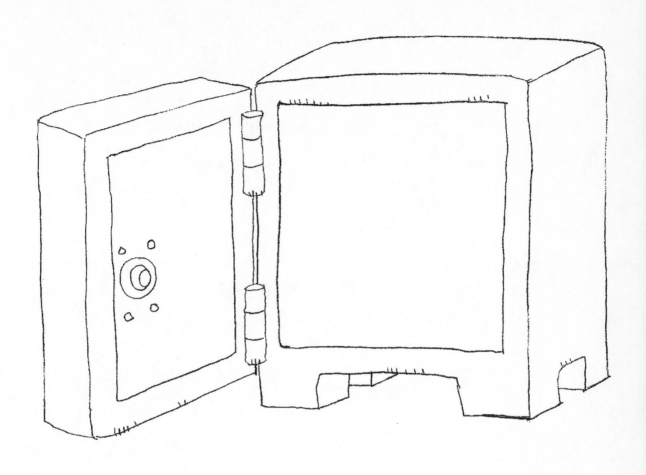

What are your secret treasures?

What's on the table?

Who are the police chasing?

Stop making that noise!

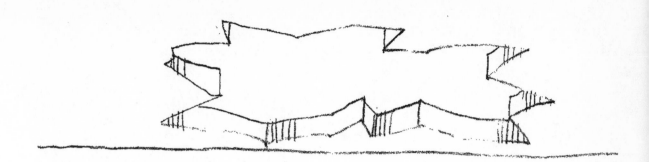

What fell through the ceiling?

The spider needs a web.

How do I get up there?

What's under the hood?

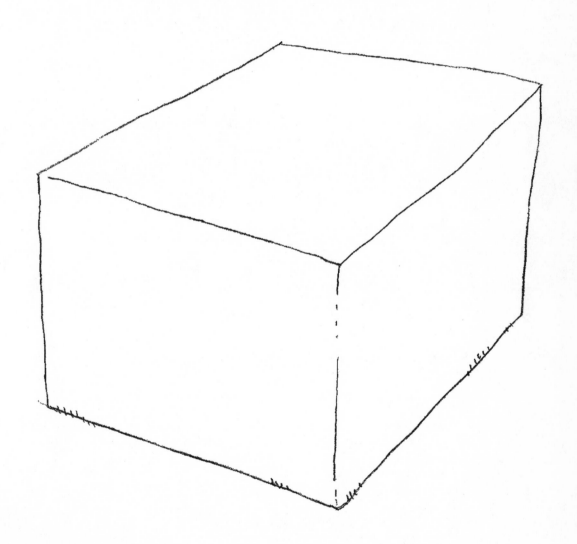

Design the trunk for all your stuff.

Why is Little Red so afraid?

What's chasing the Three Blind Mice?

That's a big baby!

What lives in the case?

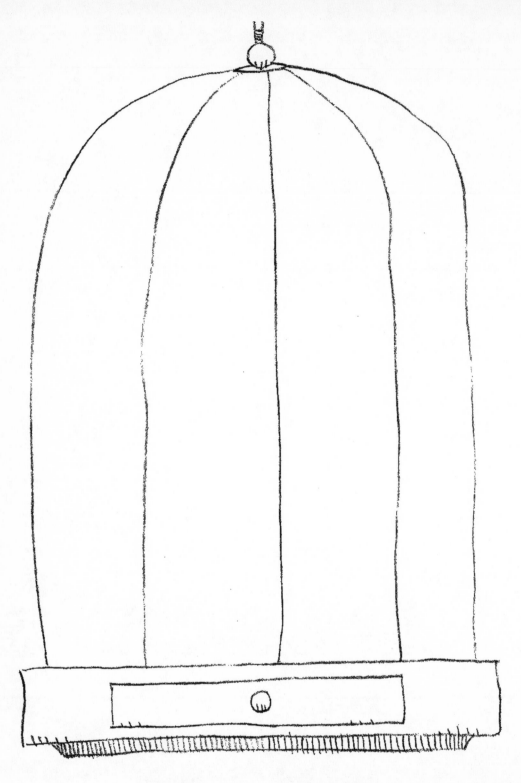

That's a really strange bird!

The famed mythical creature hunter is about to make
his greatest catch!

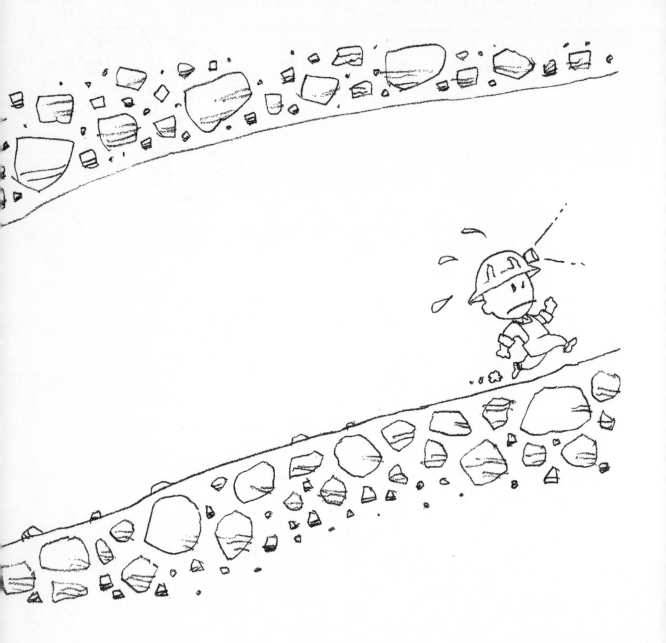

Why is the miner running?

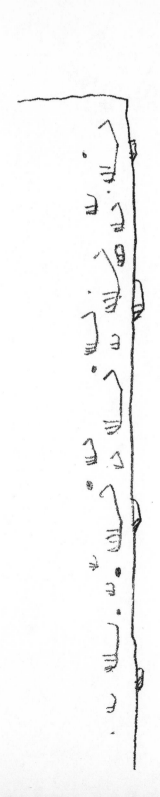
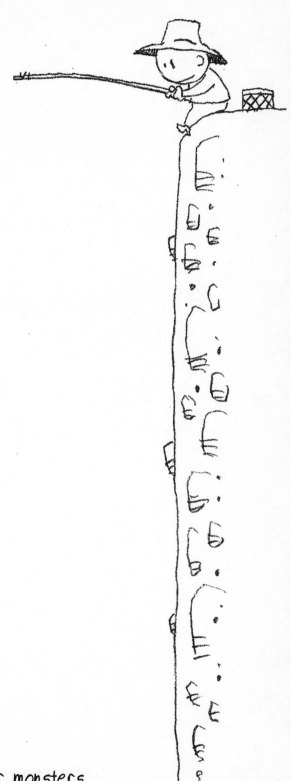

Fishing for monsters.

What's the owl hunting for?

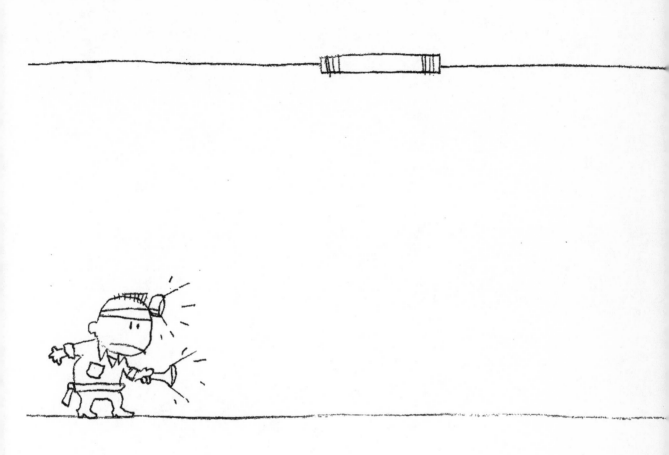

What's in the sewers?

What's the ghosthunter see?

AUGH! Rolling hedgehogs!

Wow! That's a special cone!

What's Reginald carrying for Mrs. Moneybags?

Finish the explorer's balloon craft.

Fill space with stars and planets.

Betty caught a big one!

Arrgh! I need a parachute, quick!

Give Bettie some balloons.

10-9-8-7-6-5-4-3-2-1-Blastoff!

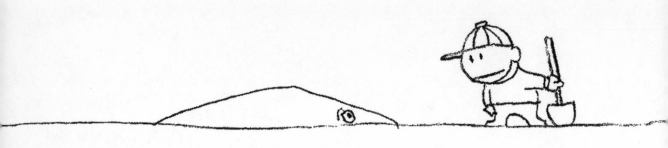

Draw the dirt monster's underground body.

Draw the picture of Dorian Gray.

What's the mouse eating?

It's a dog race.

Elvis's car is real flashy!

What did the safari photographers find?

What's in there?

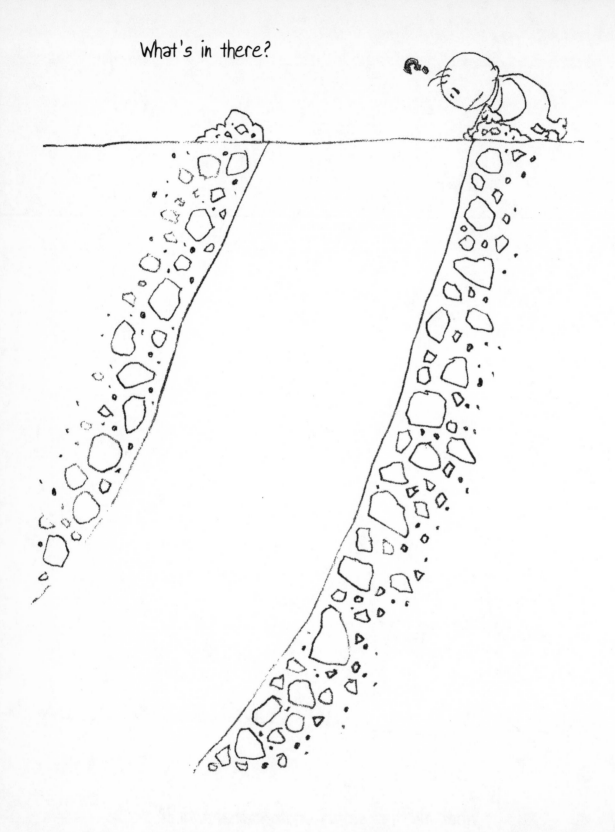

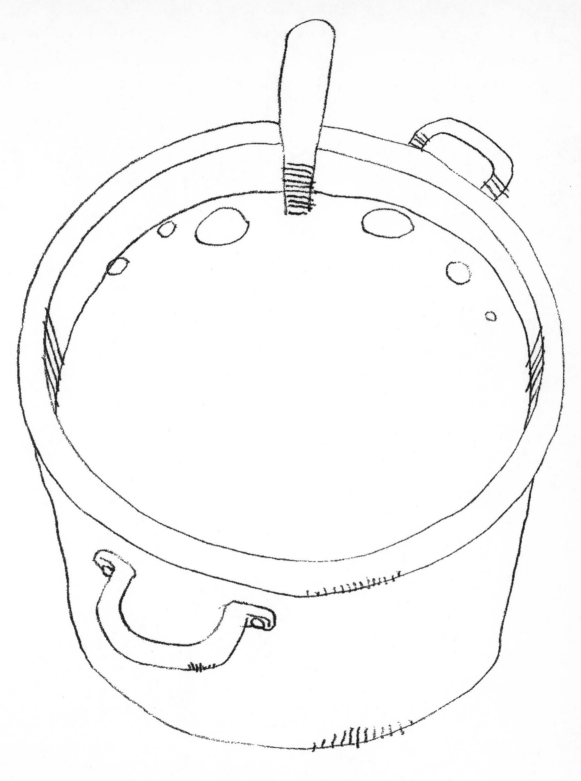

What's cooking?

Give the man a crazy hat.

It's the world's fastest motorcycle!

It's a barrel of...

Draw your dream treehouse.

What are we going to catch?

Run, Ook, run! Something's chasing you!

How's the weather in the middle ages?

Oh no! What happened to my face?!

My favorite breakfast.

Set the table for a fancy dinner.

Design your stamp.

Avast ye swabs! Where's Pirate Pete's boat?

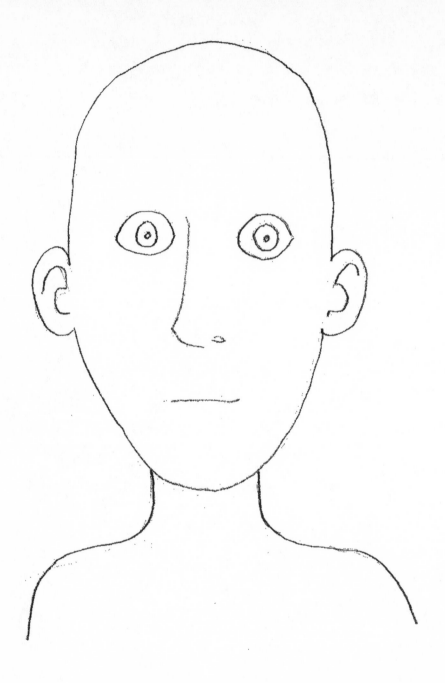

What kind of movie monster would you be?

Pop! goes the Jack in the Box.

Bug soup!

It's a rocket race!

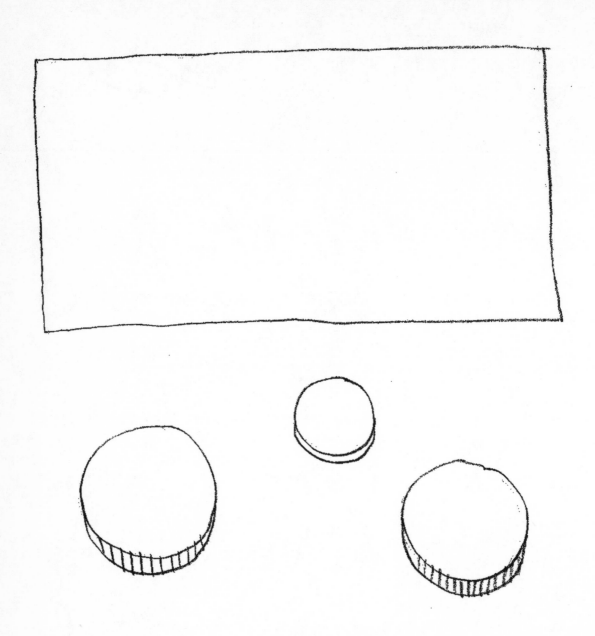

Design your money.

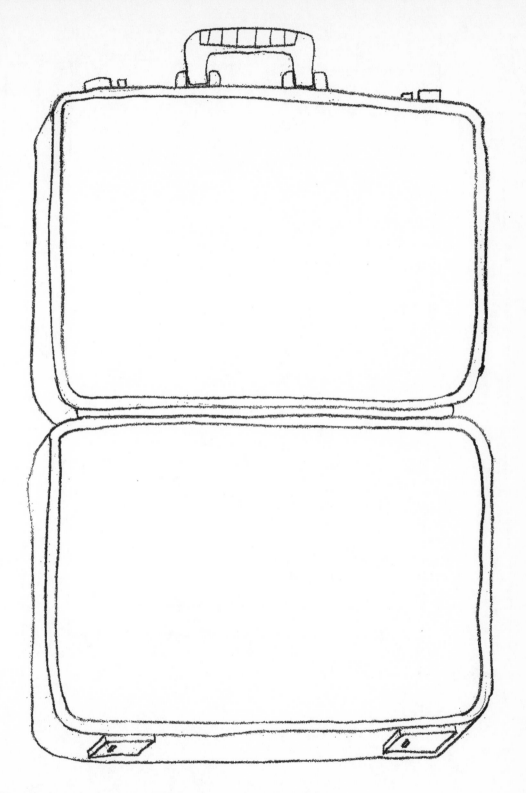

Pack for a short trip.

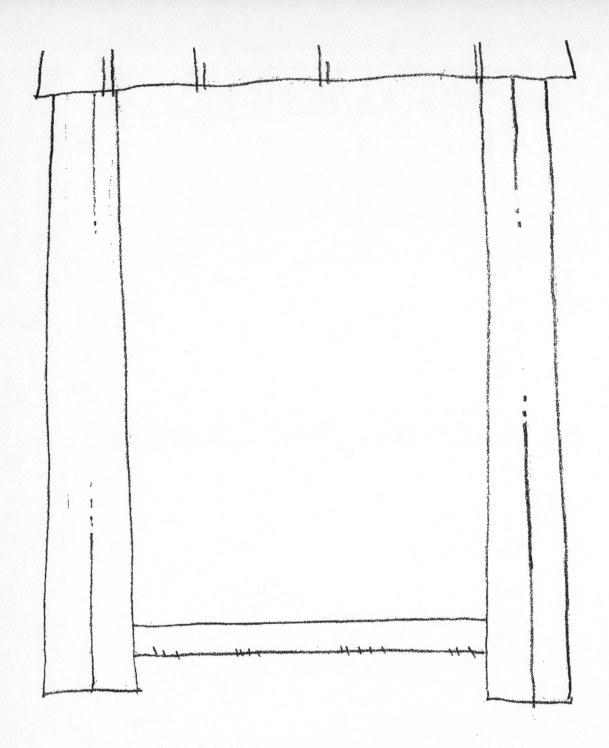

What's outside your window?

MMM! My favorite dinner!

It's the secret under the Amazon!

Give the fish some friends.

What is Granny Ninja fighting?

Hang on!

What's the scientist launching?

There's something in the deep, dark woods.

Draw a spider party.

This fruit tree needs some fruit.

What's on T.V.?